# Joyriding!

WES MAGEE was born within sight of the River Clyde, in Greenock, Scotland. Leaving school at age 16 he worked as a bank clerk and National Serviceman with the Army Intelligence Corps before training as a teacher at the University of London. Thereafter he worked in schools in Swindon, Wiltshire, before Head Teaching stints at large Primary schools in Hertfordshire and Humberside. He resigned to become a fulltime author in 1989.

Wes has published 5 poetry collections for adults, and more than 90 books for children—poetry, fiction, plays, picture books, and anthologies.

His first poetry collection, *Urban Gorilla* (Leeds University Press), won The New Poets Award (1972), and *No Man's Land* (Blackstaff Press) was a Poetry Book Society Recommendation (1978). A collection for children, *The Very Best of Wes Magee* (Macmillan) was the Choice for the Children's Poetry Bookshelf Award (2002).

He lives in Rosedale, a remote area of the North York Moors.

## Also by Wes Magee

POETRY
*Poetry Introduction: 2* (1972)
*Urban Gorilla* (1972)
*No Man's Land* (1978)
*A Dark Age* (1981)
*Flesh, or Money* (1990)
*Starfall: Winter Poems* (2005)

FOR YOUNG READERS (SELECTED BOOKS)
*Morning Break*: poems (1989)
*The Witch's Brew*: poems (1989)
*The Legend of the Ragged Boy*: picture book (1992)
*The Scumbagg School series (4 books)*: fiction (1993/4/5)
*The Boneyard Rap*: poems (2000)
*The Phantom's Fang-tastic Show*: poems (2000)
*The Very Best of Wes Magee*: selected poems (2001)
*The WinterWorld War*: fiction (2002)
*Wes Magee reads his poems*: CD (2003)
*Stroke the Cat*: poems (2004)
*Who likes Pancakes?*: poems (2005)
*Blue, where are you?*: fiction (2007)

# Joyriding!

## WES MAGEE

SALT

LONDON

PUBLISHED BY SALT PUBLISHING
Fourth Floor, 2 Tavistock Place, Bloomsbury, London WC1H 9RA United Kingdom

© Wes Magee, 2009

The right of Wes Magee to be identified as the
author of this work has been asserted by him in accordance
with Section 77 of the Copyright, Designs and Patents Act 1988.

First published 2009

Printed in the UK by the MPG Books Group

Typeset in Swift 9.5 / 13

ISBN 978 1 84471 482 7 paperback

1 3 5 7 9 8 6 4 2

'All the world's a stage,
And all the men and women merely players;
They have their exits and their entrances;
And one man in time plays many parts,
His acts being seven ages.'
   *As You Like It* (Act II, Scene VII)
   WILLIAM SHAKESPEARE

# Contents

# Acknowledgements

Thanks are due to the editors of the following literary magazines in which some of the poems first appeared: *Ambit*, *Encounter*, *Fragments*, *The London Magazine*, and *The Seventh Quarry*.

'Forty Years On' was first published in *About Larkin: The Journal of The Philip Larkin Society* (issue 19. Spring 2005)

'Dormobile Memories' was first published in *Wrecks*, a booklet of poems by Wes Magee, with photographs by Peter Barnfield published by Xenia Press, 1980.

Joyriding!

# One

I will always remember you
Entering the gate of childhood in the season
When plum blossoms give way to cherry blossoms.
— Wang Hung Kung (trans: Kenneth Rexroth)

# Laurels

They flourished in the earthy churchyard,
a profusion of bushes
beneath which children
had created pig-runs
ending in a leaf-roofed cavern,
     hidden, secret.

Nine-year-old Marion sat there,
ringlets to her shoulders
and showed her navy knickers.
The word spread.
Boys—and girls—scrambled along the runs
     to see her.

One of the greasy Jackson twins
and warty Fitzgerald told her,
 'Go on then, take 'em off,'
but Marion just grinned, showed again
the red impressions where elastic had nipped
     her white thighs.

Each Sunday that summer she was there,
concealed and silent
while parishioners
crunched along the gravel paths to church.
Reverential, we gathered to gaze,
     mesmerised, part fearful,

for to enter that dim cavern
was to witness something hallowed.
There sat Marion, a goddess,
smile inscrutable,
a crown of laurel leaves wreathing
     her long hair.

# First Love

<pre>
            I love Hazel,
    but she doesn't know it.
            How do I tell her?
                    How do I show it?
</pre>

As usual, we leave school together,
but today has an extra special glow
for—Yes!—it's the start of the Christmas break.
In freezing cold December dusk we make
our way home. As we walk it starts to snow.
Hazel, excited, says, '*Christmas weather!*'

She stops when we reach the darkened old church
and says, '*Bet you daren't walk through there alone!*'
She points to the spooky graveyard . . . so dark.
In summer we'd take this short-cut for a lark,
but now . . . in winter darkness . . . on my own?
'*Easy,*' I boast, but my heart gives a lurch.

<pre>
            I love Hazel,
    but she doesn't know it.
            How do I tell her?
                    How do I show it?
</pre>

Hazel says, '*Meet me on the other side.
Go on, Wes!*' She laughs and touches my arm.
I gulp, and push back the wrought iron gate
wondering if I'll meet some dreadful fate,
then tread the flagstone path and—in alarm!—
hear a stifled cry. I quicken my stride,

pass lichened headstones that seem set to fall
and yew trees rustling in the chill wind's moan.
I run towards the locked church, round the tower,
and race on as a clock chimes the half-hour.
Spooked, I shiver, then reach the safety zone—
the exit lych-gate. Now I'm walking tall!

> I love Hazel
> but she doesn't know it.
> How do I tell here?
> How do I show it?

I'm back on the snowy street, breathing hard,
while inside my chest my heart thumps and lifts.
I lean against a lamp-post, bathed in light,
and wait for Hazel. Now she comes in sight,
her backpack bulging with books, cards and gifts.
*'Wes, you made it!' she calls. 'How was the graveyard?'*

*'No prob,'* I croak. *'You . . . were my lucky charm.'*
Hazel steps up, takes my hand in her glove
and plants an oh-so-soft kiss on my cheek.
Spotlit beneath the streetlight I go weak
at the knees. The Christmas hols . . . and I'm in love!
As snow falls we head for home . . . arm in arm!

> I love Hazel
> and now she knows it.
> Together we walk,
> together we show it.

> Oh, *how* we show it!

## Just After the Second World War

It was a July evening, perhaps ten,
when he led her to the air raid shelter,
a blockhouse camouflaged by ivy and apple trees
at the end of a long strip of overgrown back-garden.

> They crept inside:
> a swirling cat-blackness,
> mattress-damp air,
> and then his asthmatic rasp
> before a trembling hand
> touched her blouse.

Outside again . . . the cool dark; insect drone.
They scanned the night's squadron-formation clouds,
and saw wing-tip lights of stars filling the sky.
'*Listen,*' he hissed, '*listen for the bombs.*'

> She remembered long-drawn whistles,
> dulled crumps,
> and heard now apples thudding
> in the wild grass
> as he shook boughs
> and hared away, whooping.

Through the gloom came his searchlight shout: '*I love you!*'
as from the nearby main road she heard
the sudden clang of a tram homing in,
kamikaze fashion, on the town centre.

# Two

> . . . and all those acres of bed!
> She, in attendance, wearing diaphanous,
> but never quite diaphanous enough, nightwear.
> — 'Old Movies': JOHN COTTON

# Kiss

She was so serene, her skin as smooth as an LP sleeve,
so when the students' party wound down and she made to leave

he saw her to the door. It was near dawn. They stood a sec,
he longing to touch and trace her Modigliani neck

when suddenly she turned and kissed him, languorous and soft.
Muted music soundtrack came from a back room. Someone coughed.

A motorbike tore down the road, its rip dying, then gone,
while in the star-fade dawn their doorstep kiss held on and on.

It was a movie moment, scene from a film with no name,
just a brief encounter where no one left and no one came,

her lips' full ripeness, *mmmmm*, an all-time classic in the can,
a clip he'd rerun down the years.
                                        Oh, play it again, man.

## Saturday Nights

Saturday nights found him
duffle-coated in her front room,
patient while she made her face
before they left for the Gaumont,
watching as she stashed lotions,
compact, Buddha-shaped bottles
into a vanity bag that bulged
like the body of a pregnant cat
asleep before a purring fire.

Ritualistic, the shuffling queue
until the cinema's dark claimed them.
On the wide screen Robert Mitchum's ears
were whopping as wheelbarrows.
Amidst the lianas of *Craven 'A'*
her scent was Atlantic fresh,
and ritualistic their kissing
and cuddling and nuzzling.
Nervously, her hand touched his thigh.

She shivered in the bus home.
Petrol fumes made him queasy.
An hour they stood beneath the porch,
inarticulate with frustration
until the Yale clicked with finality
and he traipsed home, jelly-legged
on the cobbles of that northern town
as Saturday reeled wearily into Sunday.
Decades on her name is a blank,

yet, this morning, smoothing lotion
into his cheeks after a wet shave,
her vanity bag is recalled.
For a moment he stands, immobile
while steam mists on the mirror
and tries to fix the memory of her face
but it is maddeningly indistinct.
Around him the world grates into first gear.
Sunday morning rituals begin.

# Stars, Sand-Dunes, Marram Grass, Sea-Thistles and Surf
*(Three Cliffs Bay, South Wales)*

A bar beside the bay
and after last orders
two teenage boys and their girls
streak along the flat sands,
barefoot and exhilarated,
shouting beneath a canopy of countless stars
until they reach the high dunes
where they scramble up,
slough their clothes in excitement
and, naked, leap and roll
down the steep slope,
sand between their toes,
sand in every orifice,
grains grating between teeth,
sea-thistles pricking flesh,
legs rasped by marram grass
until they flop at the bottom,
a gasping, laughing heap of bodies
while all around the star dome spins
and the moon weaves drunkenly
down a sea swell path,
and as surf shushes endlessly on the shore
they taste the salty tang of freedom
when all restrictions are discarded
and there is a certainty
that this shared moment,
this glimpse of joyousness
can last for ever,
for ever and ever,
world without end,
amen,
amen.

# A National Service Moment of Desire
*(München-Gladbach, Germany: 1960)*

Cunliffe returned from ten days leave in England,
     dumped his kitbag on the single, squeaky bed
and pulled out the tiniest panties they'd ever seen.
       *'Ta! Ra!'* he whooped, and pulled them over his head,
       then gobbled and sucked. His silky skull frilled with red!

Callow as cattle in that barrack-room byre
     seven virgin soldiers battled to understand
how Cunliffe had come to win that skimpy prize,
       struggled to get the picture of his one-night stand
       and the girl he'd left—bare—behind in England.

# Beforeplay

The saloon bar was raucous, tables lager-sloshed
where squad of youngsters hammered hard at getting smashed,

the laughter loud, tongues loose and glib, the jokes grown crude
as urges swelled on oxbow lakes of gassy booze.

Soon all were gagging for it in the foetid heat.
You could rename this noisy pub *The Stocious State*.

Later, on the street, frosty air's a facial slap,
and all those lustful yearnings get the sudden chop

as skimpy, crop-top girls hug tight their goose-bump breasts.
Boastful porno verbals have shrunk to squeaky bleats.

It's slowly back to single beds, all cradling aches,
sole fumblings come when keys ram home in cold Yale locks.

# Girl in the Ice-Cream Parlour
*(at Häagen Dazs in Winter Park, Florida)*

Across town a freight train was sounding
     its organ-tuning warnings
as he stepped from the sidewalk's dead heat
into a cool parlour, its red-white gleam
     clean as a freshly-cut apple

where, *'What'll ya have?'* threw him,
     as did the red-visored girl.
His, *'Ice-cream, please,'* sounded feeble.
*'Whal, we gaddit!'* and she indicated
     illuminated boards

listing everything from crushed cranberries
     to cashews and crème brûlée.
Conscious of his confusion she prepared
a mélange of melon ice, syrup,
     walnut lumps and thick cream,

a castle of confection, then quipped,
     *'Ah jus adore ya necktah!'*
Rich, he sat in the window, spooning,
while she crooned along with a country station,
     her voice a pure sound

and he was charmed by an unblemished beauty.
     Together they inhabited
an harmonious world even as, outside,
bronzed skateboarders rattled past,
     swirling the day's dust and warmth.

# On Christmas Eve

In darkness,
in an old part of town
where back-to-backs
are separated
by a narrow alley,
two half-cut teenagers
huddle against
a crumbling brick wall,
chilled lips to chapped lips,
and fondle with frozen fingers
in a graffiti-scarred domain
of trashed wheelie bins
and all-night toms.

A fanged, prowling wind
sniffs out their hiding place,
wolf-whistles, howls
as the youngsters shiver,
feet stone-cold,
at the chilling point
where an estate gang
had raped a woman
and left her bleeding,
waist naked, wasted.
Now, a solitary drunk
staggers past, mouths,
*'Focken Chrishmash!'*

Overhead, clawed stars
cling-on grimly
while a thin-bladed moon
slices fast-fleeing clouds.
The frozen teenagers meld

as across the town's rucked roofs
came peals of distant bells.
The midnight hour.
     *'Unto us . . .'*
A dog barks once.
A door slams.
In curtained bedrooms
last lights die.

# Three

My heart has made its mind up
and I'm afraid it's you.

— 'Valentine': WENDY COPE

# It Happened in the School Stockroom

It was a walk-in cupboard,
    shelf-stacked with supplies
        and a secreted bottle of gin.
            She was there, micro-skirted,
                collecting pencils for her class
                when he walked in.

Their affair was at the hunger stage.
    With door bolted they kissed greedily
        between the raffia and the rubber bands.
        Constricted, and she being small,
            they did it monkey-climbing-tree position.
            They were a Gordian knot of glands.

'*I'm coming!*' was the cry,
    and their rearing orgasm began an avalanche
        of string balls, rulers, sticks of glue.
            She emerged with throbbing temple
            and knickers balled in her fist.
                He came out punk-haired, his tie askew.

Throughout that humdrum teaching day
    she smoothed her micro-skirt
        and would not look her pupils in the eye.
        He taught class on automatic,
            licked a bitten lip, and reached
                with one robotic hand to check his fly.

# The Cure

As soon as they met
the heartache began
and both felt distinctly unwell,
*oh*, unwell.

The cure was simple
and easy to plan
—two nights at the Russell Hotel
*yes indeed*,

two nights
at the Russell Hotel!

## Love Bites

Her left breast and long nipple were bruised,
        his shoulder bitten, sore,
        when teeth and tongues were used
        to excite and explore.

Those brands ripened: midnight-mauve, through blue
        to yellow. Then . . . no trace.
        Gentler, now, their lips soothe
        each sucked and bitten place.

# Threesome

The triad dancing around the Greek urn
    arouse us with their semi-nakedness.
        Man, woman, man embrace and bend in turn,

        trail slender fingers over skin, caress.
    Sinuous, they enrapture as we gaze
and each glimpse seems to find them wearing less.

This threesome's act continues to amaze,
    the athletic positions that they hold.
        They've kept it up for, well, a million days.

        Divine *terza rima* of flesh and gold,
    the trio's jig of breast and buttock earn
our wide-eyed stare and make us horny, bold.

# First

She lit up, lay back,
and fag smoke drifted
through the thrumming gloom.
*'Was it . . . your first time?'*
Her edgy question
coiled in the closed room.

Quiet, he stared up,
tasting again the
tartness of her kiss,
and thought of other firsts:
step, word, school.
All notches, and now this.

A post-coital angst
and the acrid smoke
left him feeling arsed.
Absent chemistry
and five words ensured
their first time was their last.

# Fingertips

Gossamer, their trail-touch
left him gasping, '*Darling, it's too . . . too much!*'

Her murmurs calmed the cry.
Deft fingers dust-feathered his inner thigh.

Moth-light, she tipped his glans:
*Oh*, the resurrecting laying-on of hands.

# Afterwards

After midnight
they crept away from the party,
ventured across the lawn,
and entered a field tall with summer's growth.
The moonlight, the starlight got to them.
They made love with no frills.
Tender. Simple.

Afterwards
they leaned on a fence
and looked back to the open house.
Music. Voices. Laughter.
Long lozenges of amber light
spilled across the terrace
and its steps.

The pair
kissed again, held tight.
And then, with necks arched back,
gazed at a vast and dizzying sky.
A shooting star flared and was gone.
Tremulously, an owl cried
from the darkling wood.

# Four

Not there, but here,
(He whispers) only here,
As we are, here, together, now and here,
Always you and I.

—'Counting the Beats' : ROBERT GRAVES

# Early Starters

The humped duvet's a blue whale
beached in a drift of pillows and sheets:
        love's flotsam.
Now, downstairs at dawn,
they breakfast on croissants, tinned grapefruit,
        toast, and plum jam,

he tousled and slobby
in soiled T-shirt and baggy shorts:
        she *déshabillé*,
fiery dragons emblazoned on a silk wrap.
Their bare toes touch. She props a heel
        on his left knee.

Coffee mugs and juice cartons are shoved back
to make space for magazines and books
        amid the table's clutter.
Hushed, they frown down at the small print
of train timetables and thick thrillers.
        A knife stands in the butter.

Small sounds surround: tap's drip,
the electric wall-clock's tick, tick, tick,
        rain against the windowpane.
Their love night is over. In an hour she'll be gone,
will text from the jolting carriage
of her southbound train.

## Seeking the Seals
*(Blakeney Point, North Norfolk)*

Lovers, they plod
the shelving pebble beach,
one foot higher than the other,
each step causing a grating stoneslip,
and when they stop to shade eyes
the curved spit seems endless,
a distant shimmer of sea and sky.
Beyond that hazy beyond,
they'd been told, were seals.

Dogged, they plod on,
attuning to a new language
of wind, wave, stone and seabird.
After the night's closeness
morning freshness pumices their skin.
See them, two figures in a seascape,
yomping through vastness,
one foot higher than the other,
seeking the seals.

# Joyriding!
*(a lay-by ... after midnight)*

Car back-seat escapologists
      they fought to lose the fetters
            of jacket and jeans, shirt and shoes.
This, on a deep December night.
      Small wonder they kept their socks on!
          But how to do it? *'Your choice.'*
                         *'No, **you** choose.'*

The windows steamed and ran.
      Imprinted on their flesh
          cold steel buckle and safety strap.
A contortionist, she battled
      to wedge her legs between the seats,
          then giggled as she climbed astride his lap.

They shagged ... until a car zapped past:
      shouts, lights, horn blaring.
          The police? *'Get off! **Get off!**'* he cried.
Funked, mucky with sweat and nine-parts nude,
      they left, burning rubber.
          *'Wow, I **almost** came!'*
                    *'I nearly died!'*

# When?

She thinks
of that night
in the back
of his car
when stars
overhead
were like
glisks
in a bar.
It's days
since they spoke,
now she waits
in the hall.
O when
will he phone?
O *when*
will he call?

She remembers
his hands,
his head
on her breast.
The static
that sparked
when he peeled off
his vest.
It was . . .
nothing new
yet his lips
made her moan.
O when
will he call?
O *when*
will he phone?

# Early Morning Close-Up

The privacy of drawn curtains
and susurrations of the locker-table lamps
are backdrop to their closeness.
Face to face in the night-tousled bed
they are one heartbeat and breath.
Conjoined at nose, breast, groin and toe
a credit card would not slide between
the clammy suction
      of their juiced flesh.

Eye to hypnotic eye
they remain oblivious to the household's stirrings:
the toilet's diminuendo gush,
and that murmur of Test Match commentary
—Henry Blofeld from Pakistan, perhaps.
This is their moment of silent stasis
when all decisions can be deferred,
dilemmas left beyond
      the privacy of curtains.

# That Blanket on the Ground

Driving, he played that Billie Jo Spears oldie,
and remembered the tartan knee-rug stowed in the car boot,
forgotten in these days of air con. and fan-blown heating.
There it had lain for years, rolled, encrusted with mud
      and desiccated grass.

As the song spilled evocatively from the CD
he recalled that heatwave day spent in the Pennines
when they'd parked-up, trekked into a fir forest,
spread the blanket on a mattress of Silloth grass
      and made love alfresco.

How they'd reeked! Steamed and reeked!
Swarms of insects had homed-in on their succulence
and sent them skedaddling back to the baking car
where he'd stuffed the damp blanket, roughly.
      Its last outing.

Driving away, they'd eyed browned-off hills
and a reservoir so low that drowned barns were resurfacing.
The blanket was history. On its faded check
their juices dried, along with soil, sap,
      and milk of crushed grass.

# The Letter

Occasionally, at close of working days,
they'd quaff a lager in a local bar
then linger over goodbyes at her car
before they drove off home their separate ways,

he married, she so gamine, just workmates
until the moment when their fingers met.
The car park saw them kissing in the wet.
Desire, an ache, gave rise to furtive dates

but then a letter stunned him at his desk,
anonymous, a threat to tell their boss.
Shown the sad scrawl, the smitten girl felt loss
when he said they were putting all at risk.

Someone had sussed their yearning, someone knew
and down long years the question bugged them

*. . . who?*

# Five

& I put Miles' *Sketches of
Spain* on the stereo & we
had popcorn that night, 7-
up, & made love on the
livingroom rug.

— 'Don't Shoot': WILLIAM WANTLING

# Love on a Mountain Top

Past the tree line they tracked a mountain stream
which gargled around boulders and was plugged,
in one peak-pictured pool, by a drowned ram.
Then squelched slow through pockets of peaty bog,
cleared the brow, strode to the stone-strewn summit.
There, a rattling cairn on which they plonked rock.

Higher than any living thing in sight
they spread plastic macs, stared at crags, chewed cheese,
and later made love, jeans shackling their feet.
The wind fumbled his buttocks: hers were pricked
by frost-fractured fragments of that rough bed.
Air was lemon-juice sharp. They came quickly.

She added panic to his paced-out heart
imagining some crimson-cheeked climber
stumbling upon them as his genitals shrank.
His bonhomie would have been misplaced!
Descending, as the light died, they paid out
yards of chilled air between them on the scree.

At the trees again they came together.
Darkness was drawing up its trews. Beneath
the dense pines an intangible gloom roosted.
He recalled nights when parents moved with stealth
in their bedroom, the pillow-stifled gasps,
and felt now a needling sadness, a guilt.

# Iris

She's so well-named.
The iris of her emerald eye
is flecked with autumn's ferny fawn.
She's enchanting for that alone.

And there's yet more to desire:
flower-like the petals of her vulva,
and her sphincter's secret iris
that trembles open at a touch.

Like a vase of slender irises
coming to bloom in a sun-filled room
her scent trail is seductive,
draws you towards her welcome.

## Where the Bee Sucks

In the garden
    one day sunny
        when their skin
            with sweat was slick,
           they spread honey
      on each other
    and gave hours
of suck and lick.

             As bees buzzed
          deep into flowers
      tipsy on
    the taste of honey,
    they gave lick and suck
      for hours
        in the garden
           one day sunny.

# Footsie

The dinner party was progressing well
and ties and talk had loosened
by the time profiteroles and sorbet arrived.

He freeze-framed on a spoonful
when her bare toes touched his shoe
and crept up a trousered calf,

and as she reclined and licked lips
her outstretched foot inched along his thigh
to brush a bunched groin.

Transfixed on her dangly earring
his look was that of the surprised celebrity
caught mid-spoon by a paparazzo,

while down the long table
liqueurs were lipped lasciviously
and tongues wrapped around mint chocs,

and still the footsie game went on,
her toes secretly manipulating and massaging
while cream drooled from his open mouth.

# That Other World

    Strangers, they gathered for a writing course
at a remote country house and discovered
there would be no TV, newspapers,
or radio for the week. Clearly they must
show an interest in each other's problems.
Dismayed, some swigged whisky in their rooms.

    The tutor enjoined them to step into,
'that ... that other world ... the imagination' ... ,
and spoke at length of the 'creative process'.
Piles began to itch, but the landscape was rich
and by Day Two they'd explored the wood,
forded a river, and scribbled fitfully.

    Laughter was heard across fields: someone sang.
A jovial sun joined in the cerebral flush
but night created a different world of 'other'.
One man stripped beneath the stars.
In the barn two figures touched. A lady, sixteen again,
was liberated amidst daisies and grass.

    It was like an Irish Murdoch novel:
musical beds more popular than charades.
Too soon it ended. They swapped addresses, kissed,
and promised to write. Leaving, they caught cricket scores
on the car radio. Thus, another life intruded.
On rear seats empty bottles chinked and chimed.

## Mise en scène

Backdrop: night sky, stars,
streetlights suspended
like flying saucers.

A darkened bedroom,
velour drapes parted,
wicker chairs, cushions.

At the long mirror
a spider holds, shifts
one millimetre.

Lozenges, tablets
on the headboard shelf,
gin in a tumbler,

and, mesmeric green,
digital clock glows.
Radiators tick.

Concealed beneath a
tumbled duvet—socks.
Strewn—bra, tie, trousers.

On the tousled bed
two lie after love,
and the scene is set

for tentative words,
lines and dialogue,
a brief kiss, exits.

# In Bed with the Cuddly Creatures

She was an animal lover,
her swagged and tasselled four-poster bed
a nest for soft toys and cuddly creatures
— panda, lion, gonk, tiger, stuffed snake, and Ted.
    That bedroom was a perfumed boudoir
where joss-sticks threatened the smoke alarm
and pot-pourri smouldered in Victorian gazunders.
She wore rabbits' fur gloves — erotic charm —
        to strip her man before the full-length mirror.

Their lovemaking was fast and furious,
a feral mating, all nails, teeth and bear hug,
while squashed cuddly ones performed as back supports
or ended-up glassy-eyed on the sheepskin rug.
    Once, as the lovers ground towards *le petit mort*,
the door burst open and in crashed
her Yorkshire terriers, Boycott and Scargill.
Now *this* was their game: they trashed
        the soft toys: kapok strewn across the floor.

The dogs leapt on the hot writhers,
blunt claws raking his back and thighs,
long tongues rasping buttock and breast
while her strangled 'No! No! No!' cries
        were lost in a tumult of growl, snarl, yelp, and bark.
And in that bedroom's storm-tossed restlessness
all was ravelled, all rucked
where one long-drawn orgasmic '*Yesssssssssss!*'
        erupted from the wrecked bed's Ark.

# Six

Say I'm weary, say I'm sad,
Say that health and wealth have miss'd me.
Say I'm growing old, but add,
Jenny kiss'd me.

— 'Jenny Kiss'd Me': LEIGH HUNT

# Butterfly

For her 50th birthday
     she's gifted herself a tattoo
          of the lepidopteran kind,

        a buttock-based butterfly
    seen only by her lover
when he takes her from behind.

## Love in the Bath

Submarining in the bay of the bath
      he's idling in foam. Periscope up! Here
she comes wobbling and steaming into port.
      He watches her stow unwanted gear

then steer straight for his landing-stage.
      Tugging, he snags a toe in the plug—*shtick!*—
but now's no time to fret, she's here,
      slippery with soap and blowing hot for her Moby Dick.

Ah, *this*—no pleadings needed—
      is what he's trawled for, and who cares about her
cod eyes and spare lifebelt? It's down anchor
      with hands plunging for buried treasure,

wanting to loose the catch on her engine room hatch.
      So, there he is, deliciously afloat, with a hold on
her limpets and torpedo running hard on course.
      In a sudsy grey wash he mines her golden

gate and a sea scent floods his mouth.
      Alive and flowing, the oceans swell with fusion
                  way
                      down
                          south.

## Skin Flick

Milky cats,
the nudes purr,
slow-stroke
legs and breasts
with delicate fingers.
Lips linger long on lips.
Erotic with breathing,
the air swells blue.

On leaving,
swing doors sigh.
In the bare foyer
usherettes stand slinky
in see-through smocks,
dandling torches
and sucking hard
on aniseed balls.

# Rodin on the Underground

It's late.
A tube train rattles deep beneath London,
and in the carriage's unforgiving glare
two are entwined across an armrest.
Weary passengers affect not to see the pair
who remain sealed mouth-to-mouth between
King's Cross and Russell Square.

Out on the echoing platform they stand
— still from a Fifties' film noir shot in half-light,
as solid and dovetailed as Rodin's *The Kiss*.
Glazed eyes view this sculptured sight
before grating doors slam shut
and the train jerks off into stygian night.
It's late.

# Bathtime

The door is locked,
  six candles glow,
    a CD wails,
      the foam's like snow.

      Steam is rising,
      waters swirl.
    The drift of hair,
  the pubic curl.

One rubber duck,
  one phallic boat,
    an ocean scent,
      her breasts afloat.

      The silken skin,
      oils so smooth,
    bubbles swell
  and lotions soothe.

Eyes are closed,
  and feet propped-up.
    Private time.
      Hands that cup.

      The door is locked,
      six candles glow,
    a CD wails,
  the foam's like snow.

## Top Shelf

On a bedroom shelf, at tiptoe reach,
they keep a copy of *The Joy of Sex*.
Plain brown paper wrapped it stands between
her *Fear of Flying* and his *Life* of Becks.

Regularly they viewed the couplings
— the mussed, damp-haired woman, that bearded bloke.
Positional skills were serious stuff,
not mere grind for some comic's filthy joke.

Years they practised rubber contortions
until pulled muscles, groin strain stopped all that.
Now they find comfort in Jane Austen,
coffee, Christmas cards, and stroking the cat.

# Physical Geography

I.

Questing, she cruised his coastline,
found a promontory, landed,
planted her flag, and laid a claim.

Meanwhile, he climbed rounded hills,
stumbled upon a lush valley,
damp and smelling of vegetation.

Together they lovingly explored
each curve and contour,
inlet, island and isthmus,

then ventured with trepidation
into the dark interior
to discover a garden of creation.

## II

The years eroded their togetherness.
Earth tremors set in, cracks appeared
before a Richter scale quake

wrecked the landscape,
and time's tectonic drift
dragged their continents apart.

Separation found them alone
on distant shores, gazing back
across a gulf flooded with salt water.

Irreversible, time's march.
There was no going back. Now,
above their heads, the wheeling seabirds cry.

## The Miles . . . the Miles

There were miles between them . . . miles,
so they came to rely on emails to warm their affair,
a relationship rekindled by mini-breaks
spent at small hotels in stone towns where
they shared stolen hours. On private nights like these
the embers of their passion would briefly flare.

But it was the computer where they'd mostly meet,
those countless chatty emails stored in files
listing the minutiae of their lives—what the cats did,
work gossip, how a roofer's due to fix the tiles.
As the hours turned into weeks, months, years,
their love-flame flickered still despite the miles . . . the miles.

# Seven

... sans everything.

— *As You Like It* Act ii. Scene vii: WILLIAM SHAKESPEARE

## Dormobile Memories

*Such* a time she had that summer
parked in the shadow of sand-dunes
while the sun dissolved in the sea.
*Oh*, such nights when naked figures
wrestled hard in their sleeping bag,
and her tin sides perspired with love.

Abandoned, she stands held fast by bindweed,
skin peeling where the suntan fades.
Her tyres have sagged, her nipples rusted.
Once she was a lovers' nest on wheels
but now squeaking springs are sole reminder
of *such* nights when her world bucked and sang.

# Forty Years On

*What will survive of us is love.*
　　　　　　　　— 'At Arundel Tomb': PHILLIP LARKIN

### I.

Teenagers, they fumbled in the cinema's back row
and, one iced night in the dead of winter long ago
when totally togged-up in duffle-coat, scarf and glove,
they clung and trembled beneath a dripping, humpback bridge.
A passion play rehearsal performed inside a fridge!
So, what became of her, his mini-skirted first love?

### II.

Forty years on just one phone call had him seeing stars
—Venus must *surely* have been in conjunction with Mars—
and they rendezvoused in that same town: she now long-skirted,
he greying and rotund. They lunched in a pub, rambled
non-stop through four decades of lifestyle news, then ambled
around a ruined castle. Like teens, they flirted.

### III.

And it came to pass, at the far end of middle age,
a five-star hotel's four-poster bed was the soft stage
for a grand performance of their synchronized sex show.
And who cared about stomach bulge, sag, or wrinkly face?
It was like a comet coming back from deepest space
to be greeted with orgasmic cries of '*Wow!*' and '*Oh!*'

IV.

And today? Another decade's almost come and gone
and assignations in chill, distant towns just aren't on.
Passions have cooled to postal gifts: silk scarf or suede glove.
Those fumbling, unrhymed efforts when the weather was hard
have shrunk to trembly one-liners of the Christmas card:
*'Memories . . . and good wishes for the coming year. Love . . .'*